Christmas Coloring Book For Kids

Hours Of Coloring Fun For Children Of All Ages

Zen Journal Team

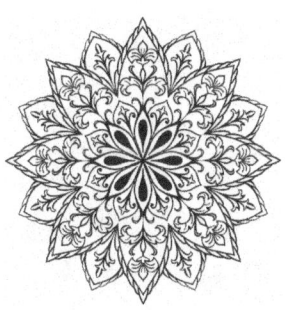

This Book Belongs To:

_____

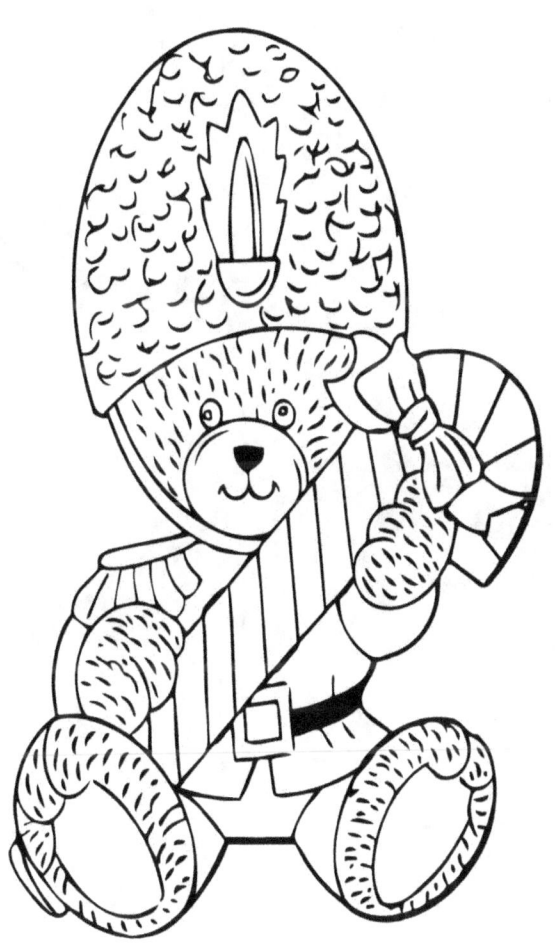

Santa's Reindeer Are Excited!

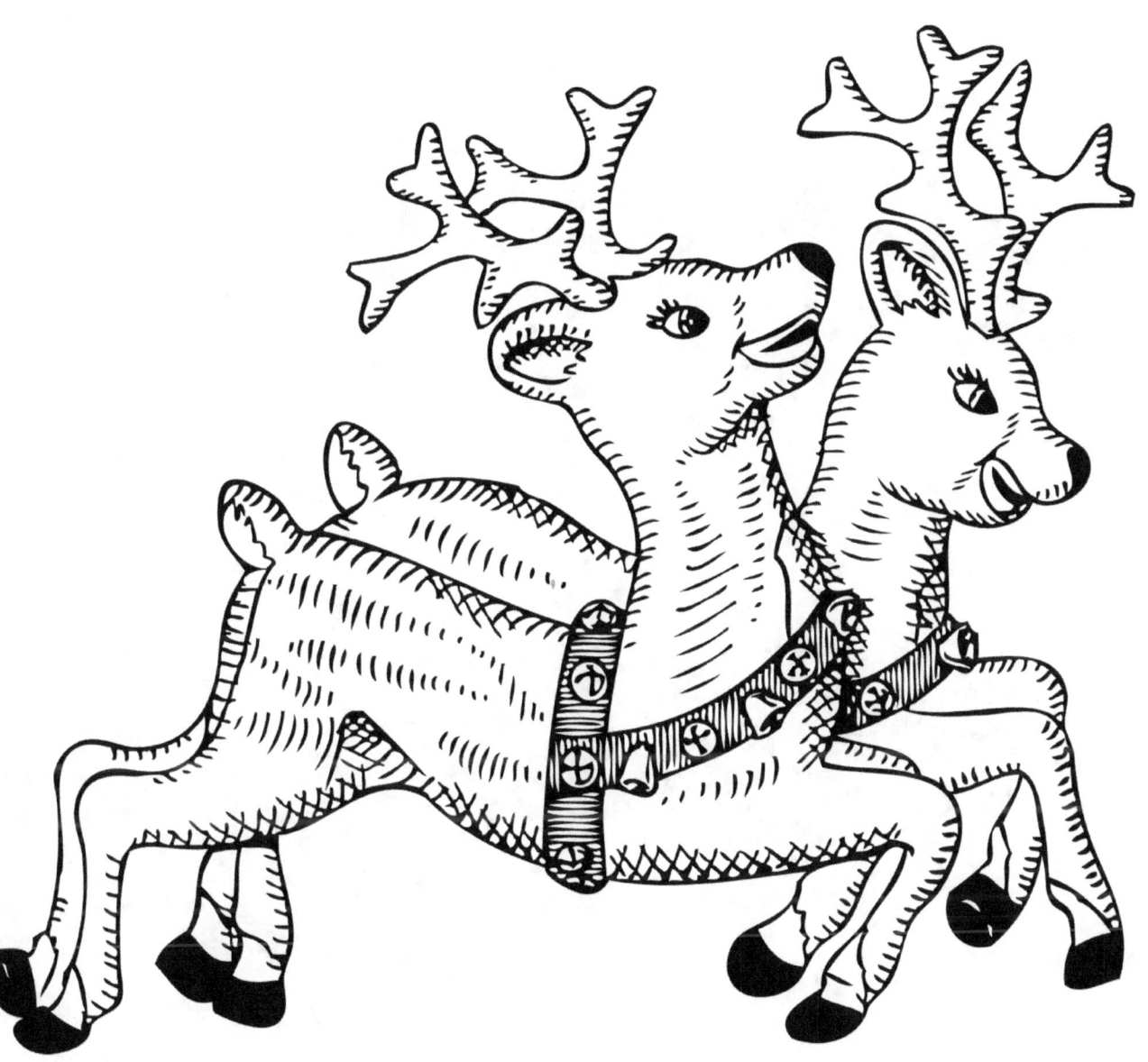

Do You Know Why?

Children Are Whispering Secrets

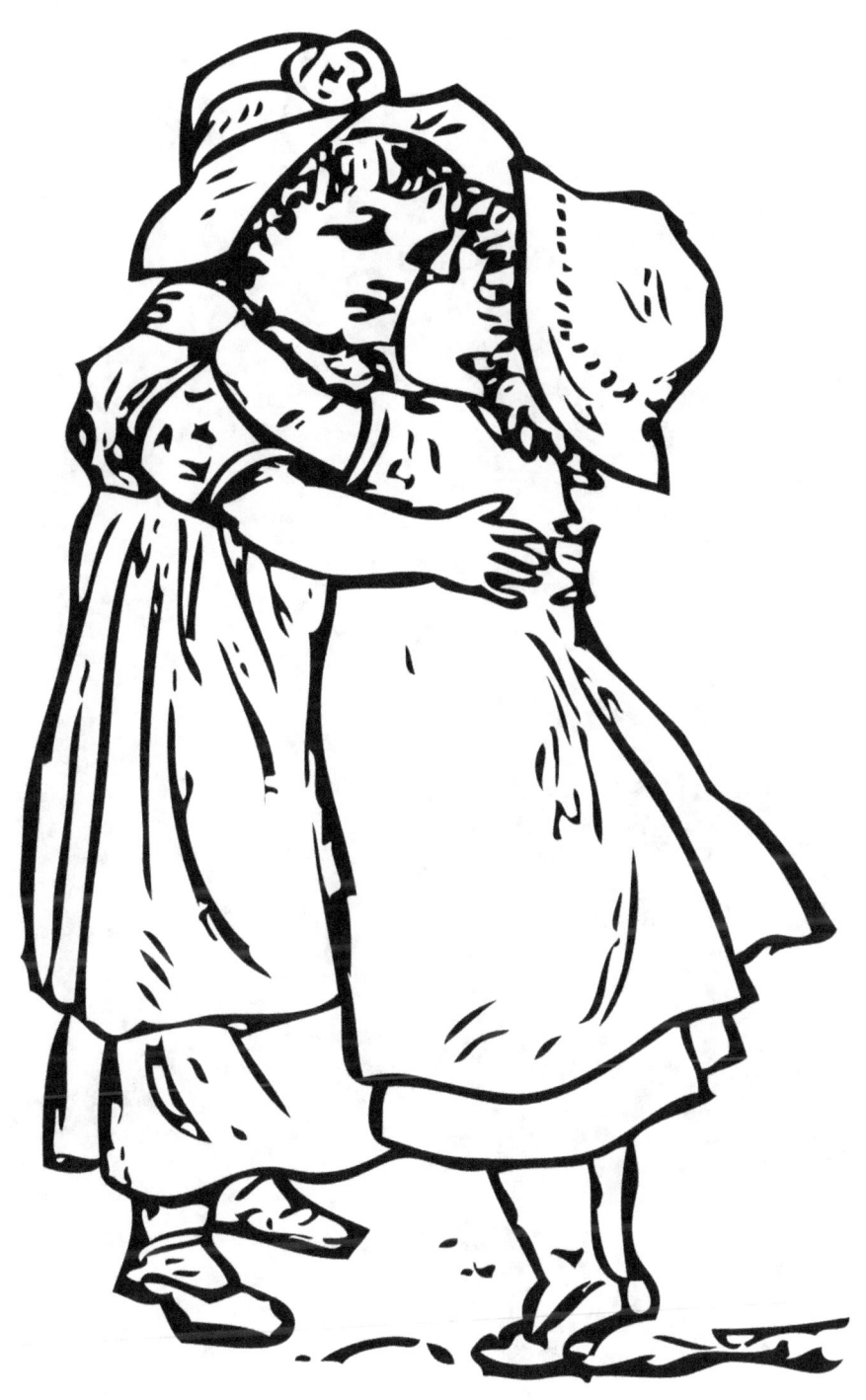

And Looking Up To The Sky

Snowflakes Are Falling!

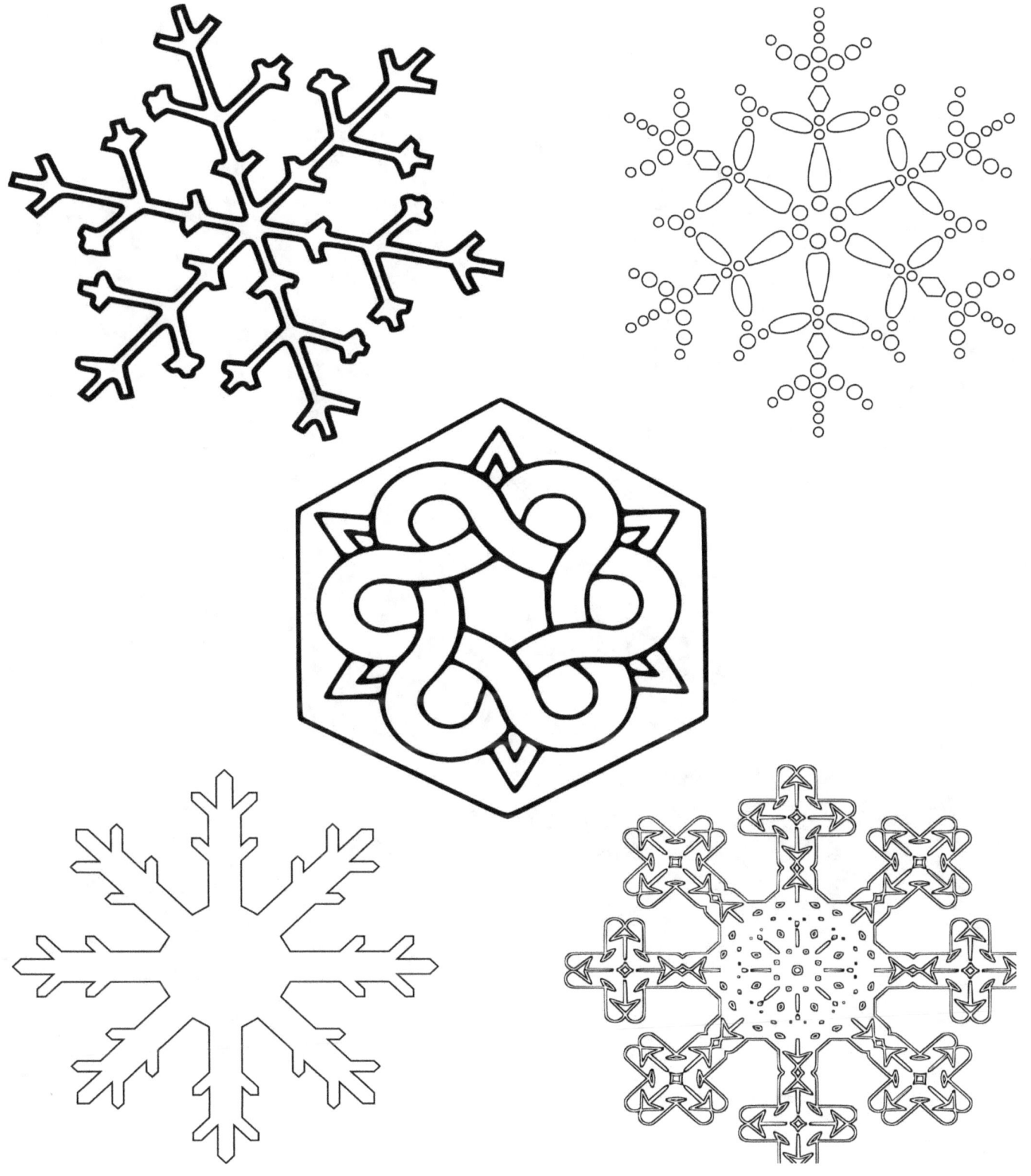

There's A Chill In The Air!

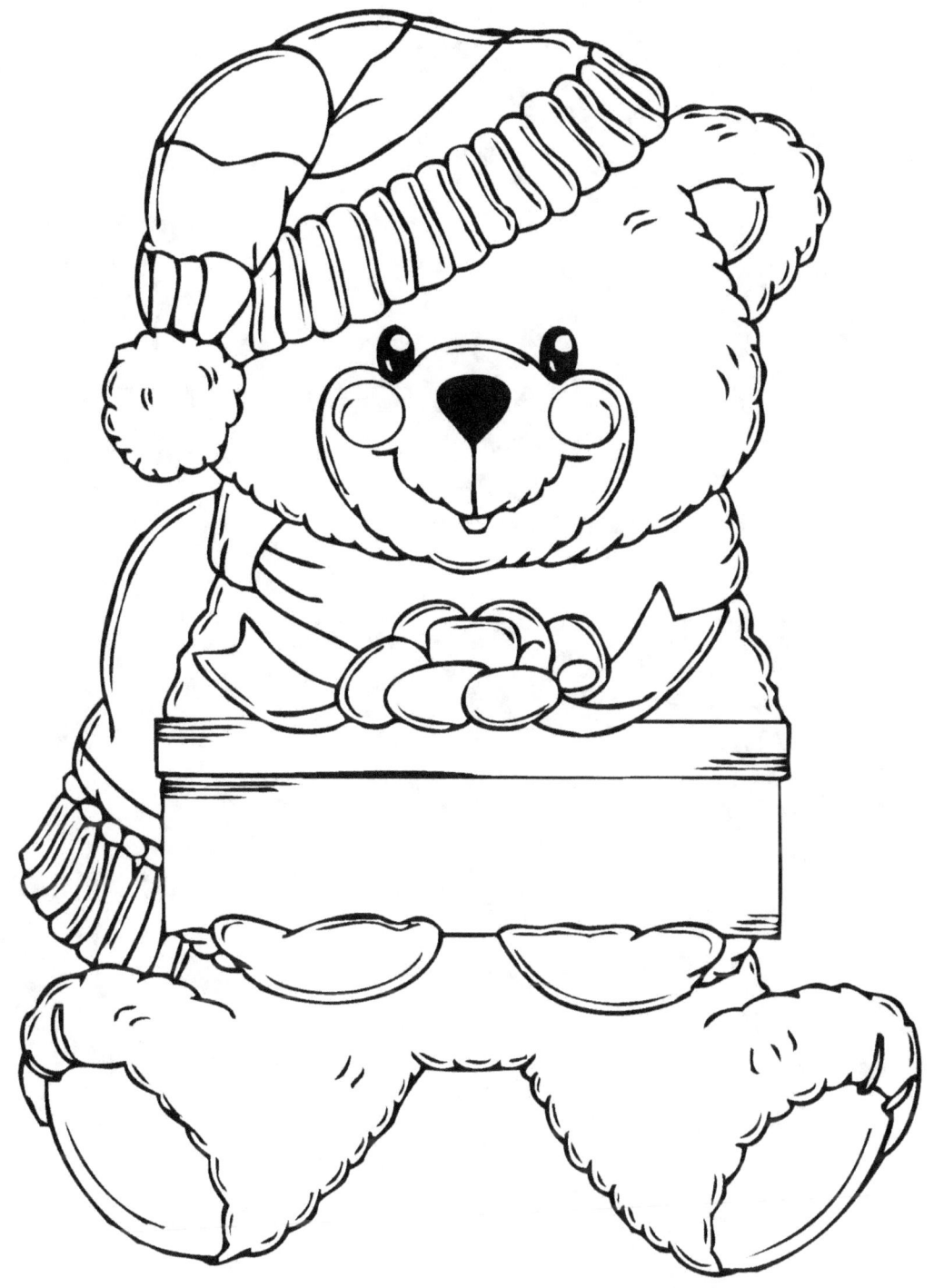

It's Winter Coat Time For This Little Bear!

Santa's Getting Busy!

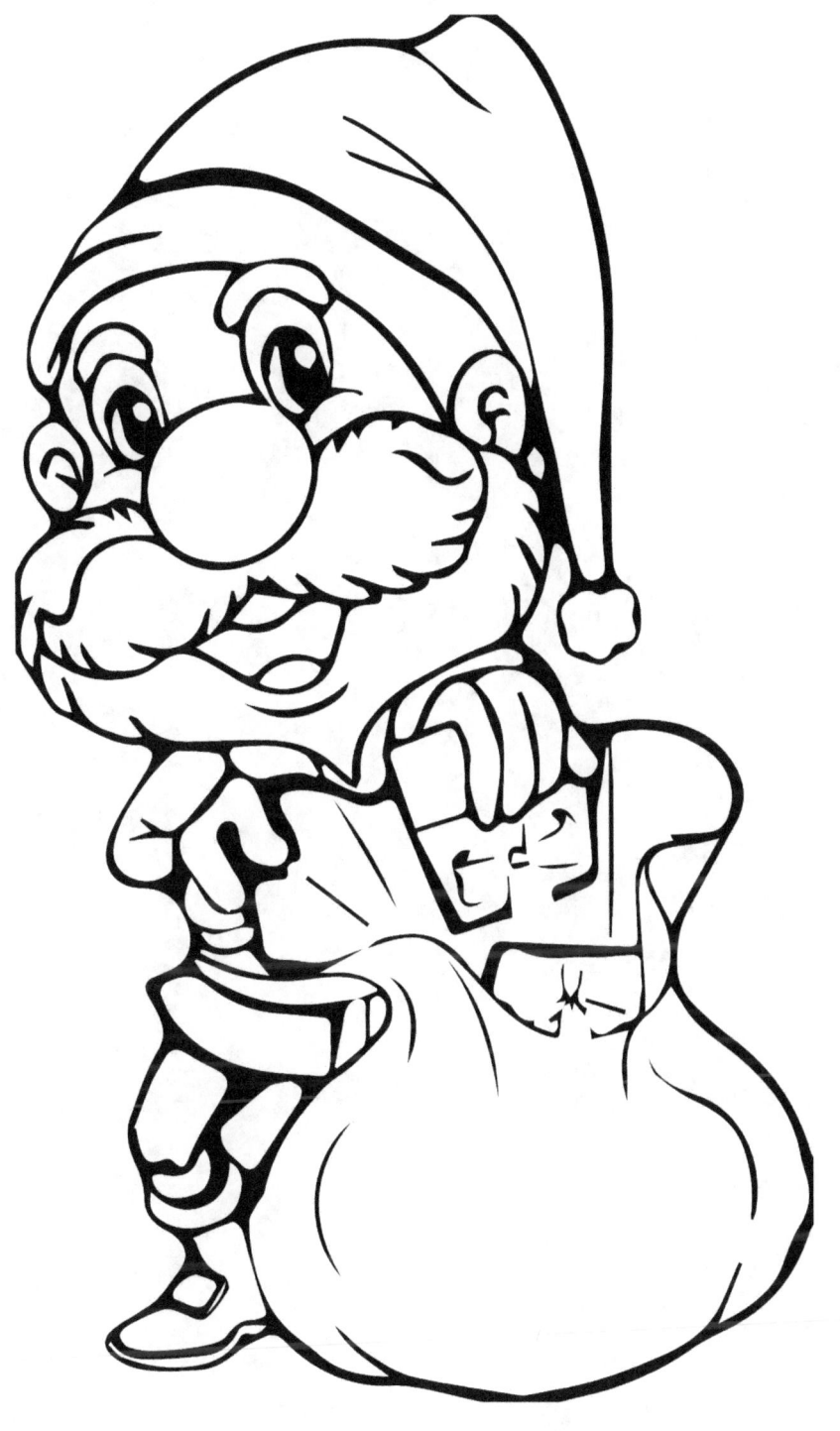

The Elves Are Too!

Making Lots Of Toys And Presents

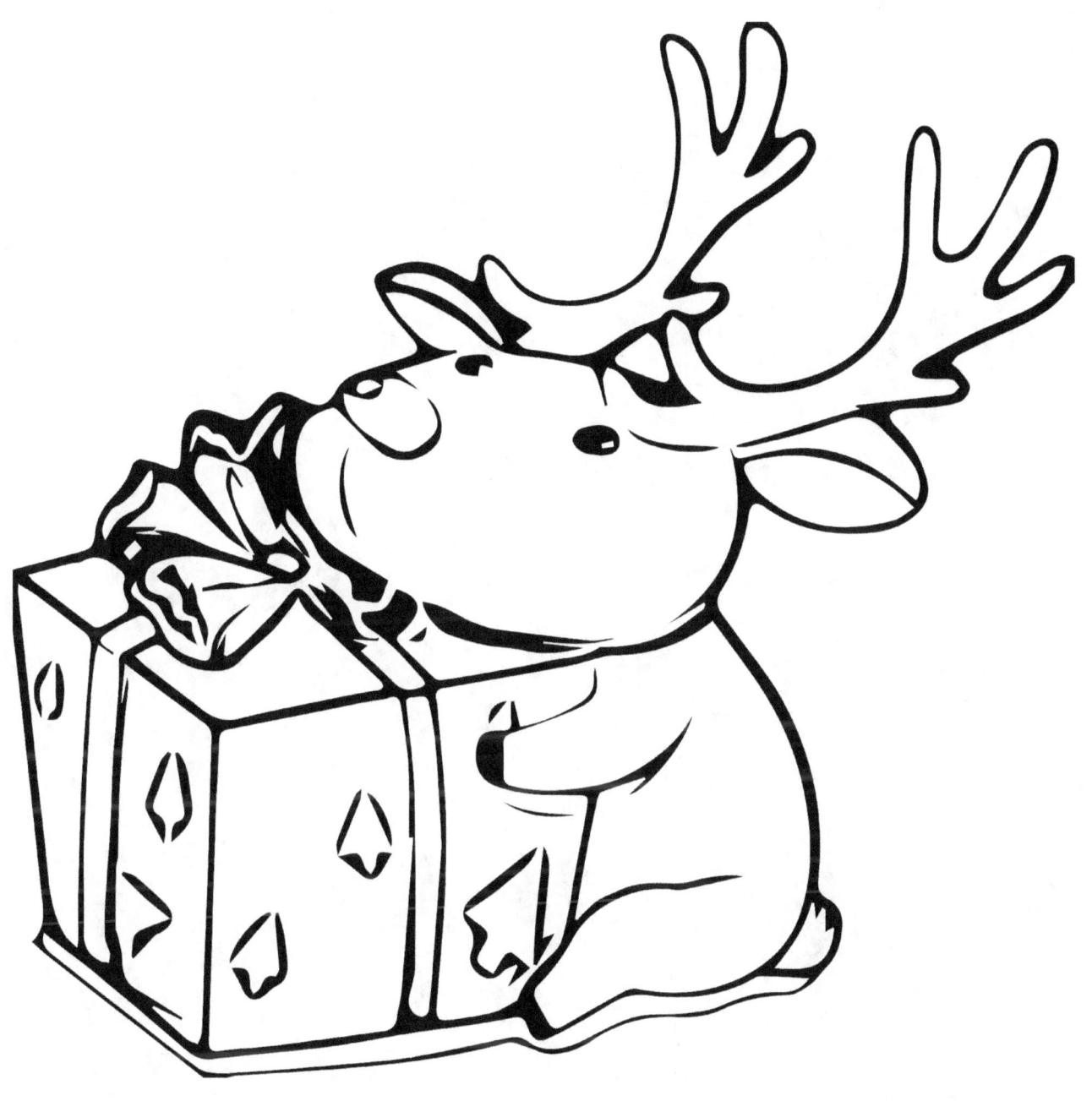

For Girls And Boys Just Like You!

Here's Smiley The Elf

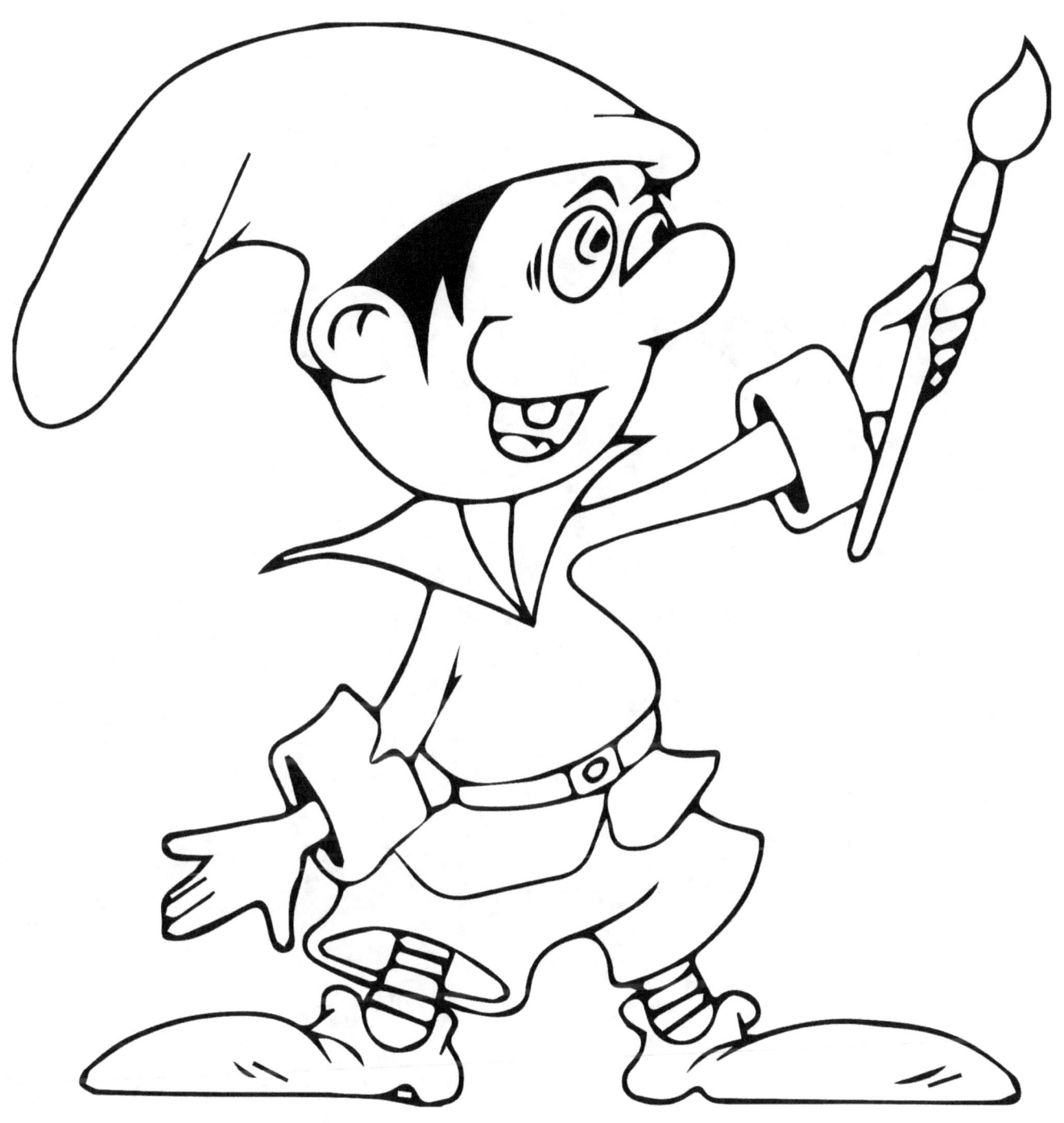

He Loves To Paint And Sing,

And Here Is Jimmy The Elf...

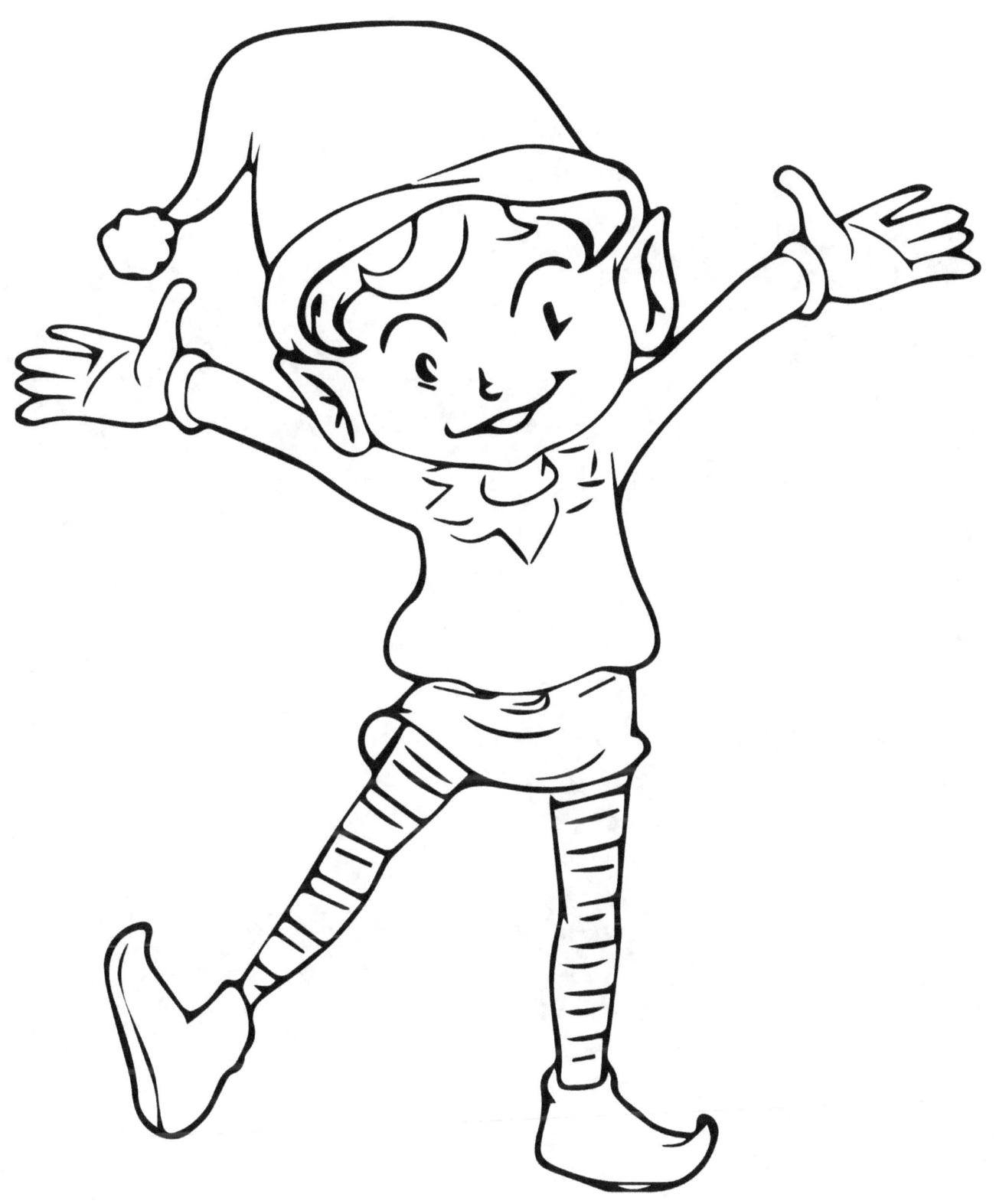

He Likes Making Presents For Santa to Bring!

Katrina Elf Loves to Dance And Play,

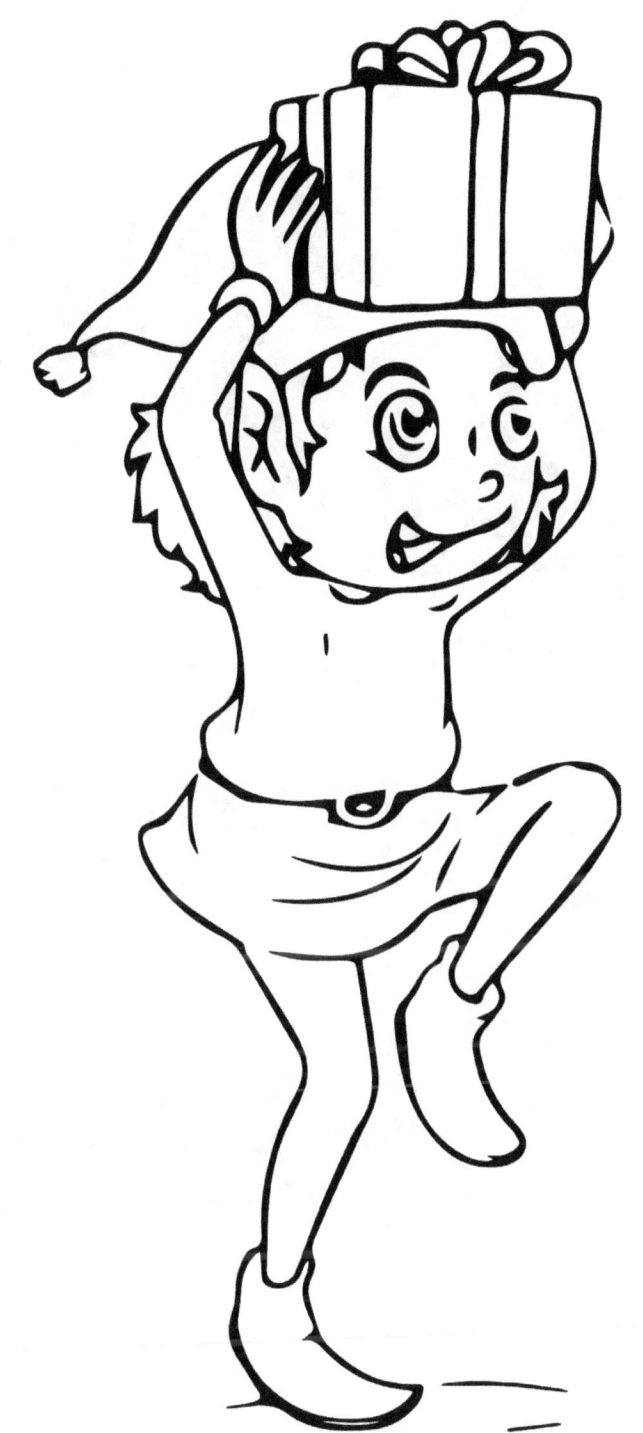

She Just Can't Wait For Christmas Day!

Look There's Rudolph Reindeer
And His Sister Rose!

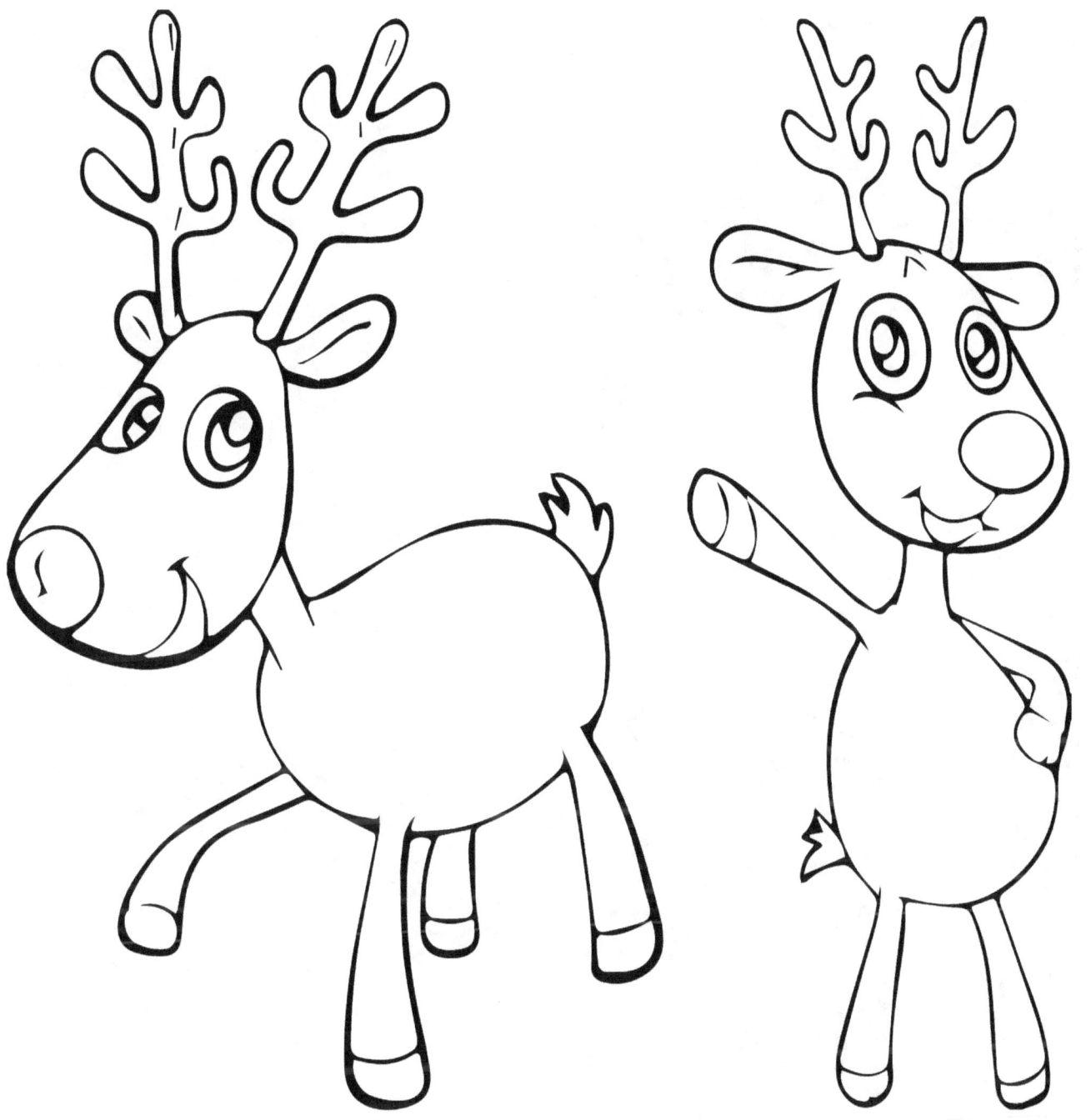

And Just Like Her Brother Rudolph
She Has A Big Red Nose!

Have You Made Your List Yet
Of Presents YOU Would Love?

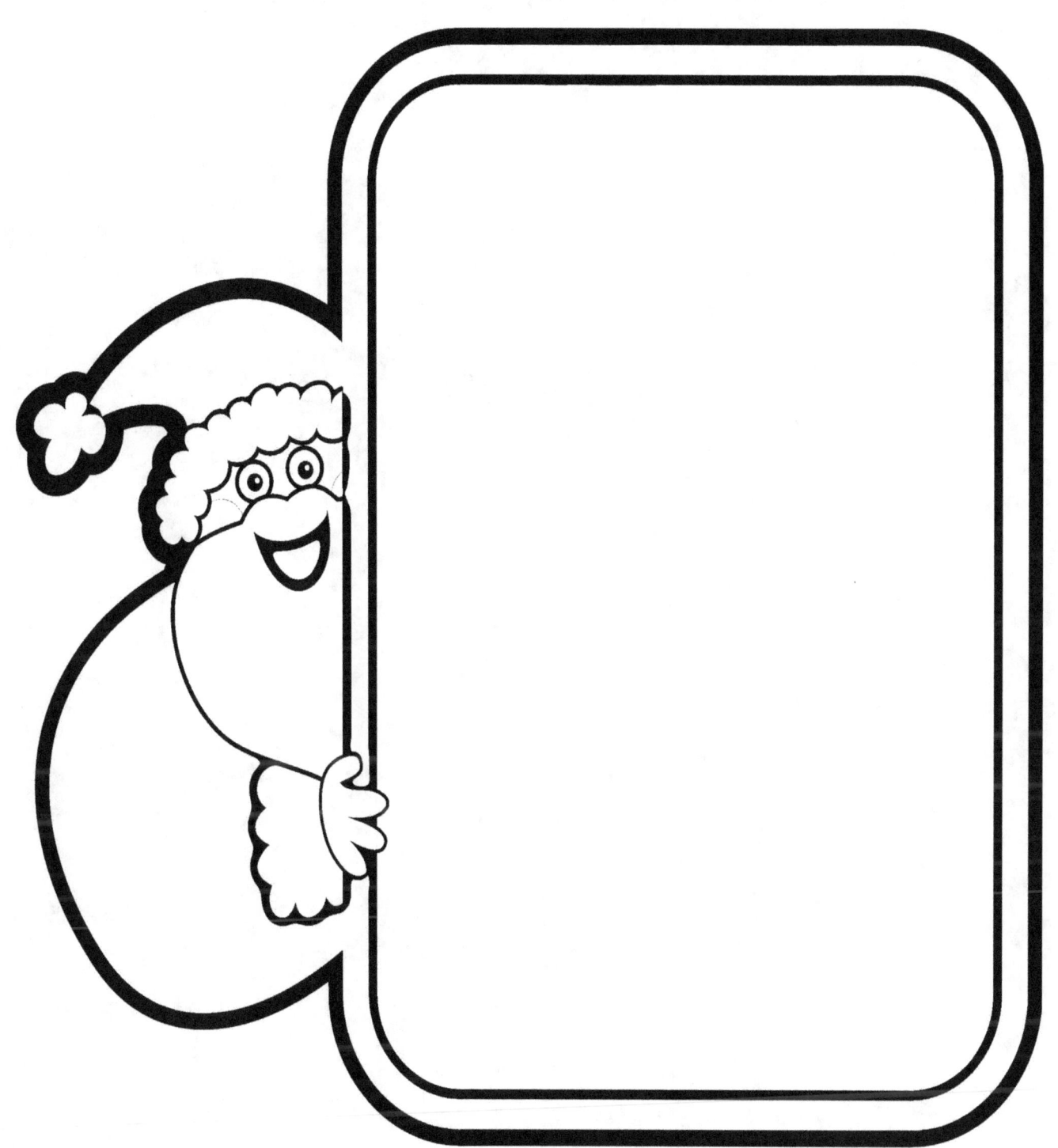

Better Write It All Down Here And
Send To Santa With YOUR Love!

So Help With The Decorations...

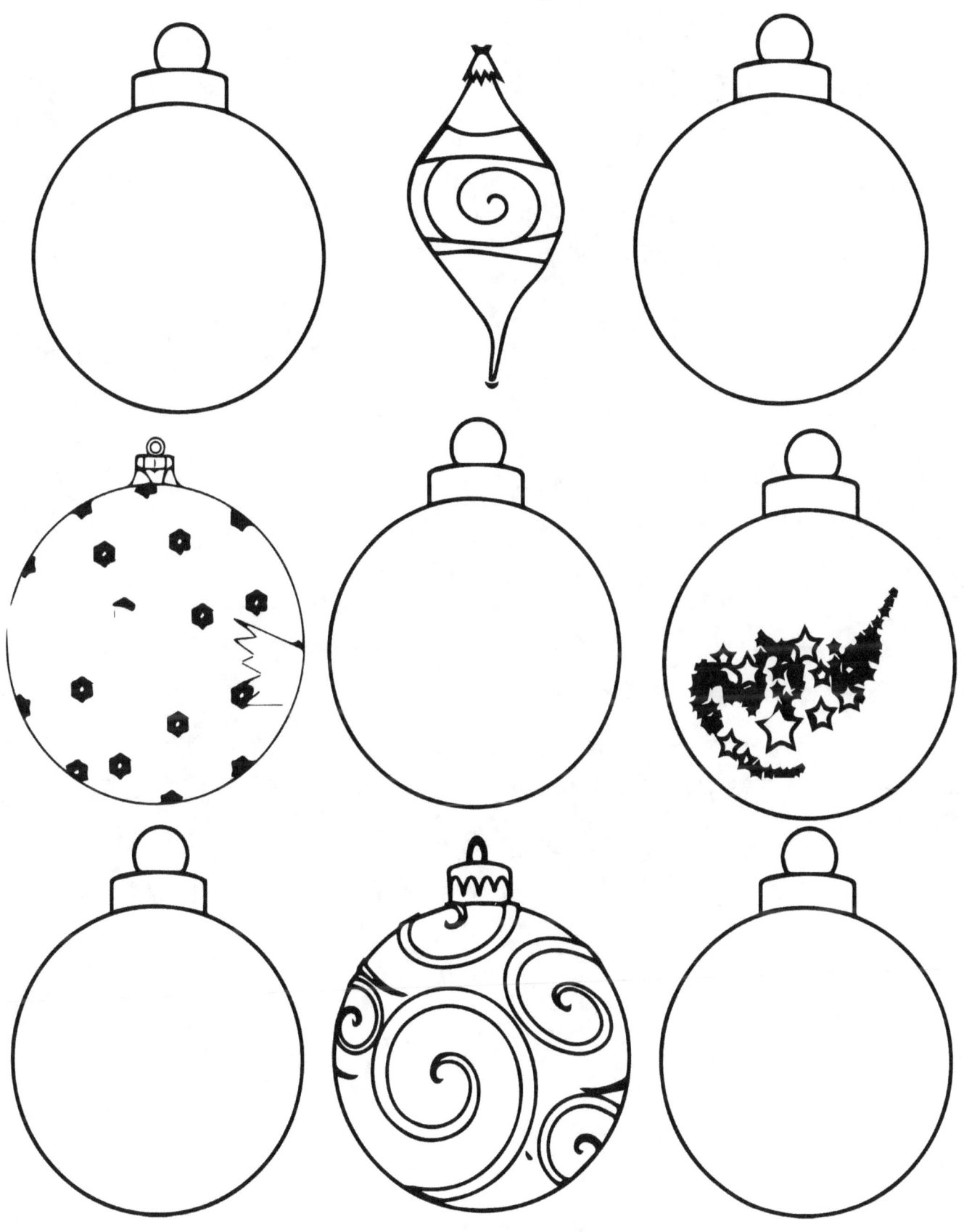

And Help Put Up The Tree...

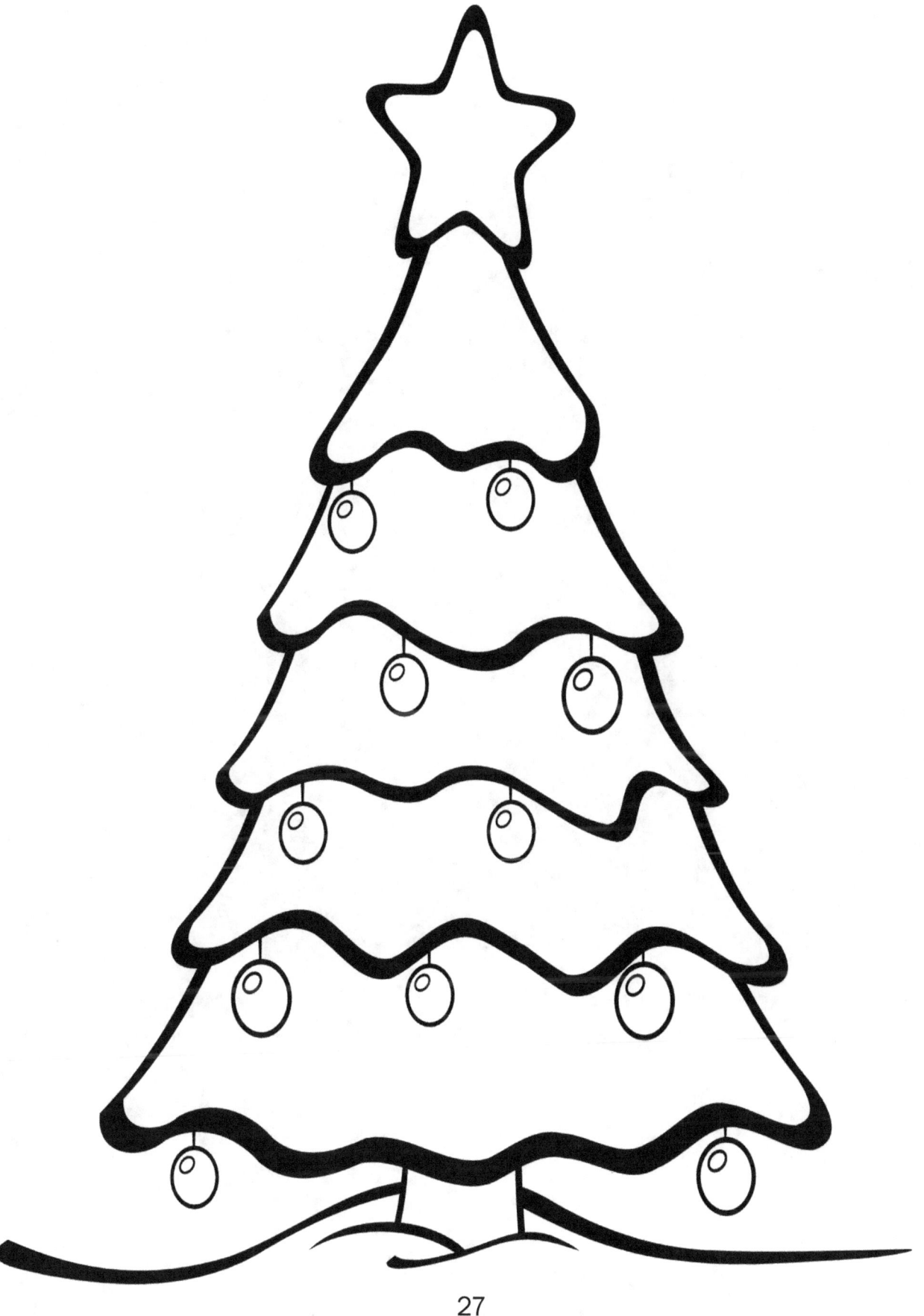

Watch Out For Flying Reindeer

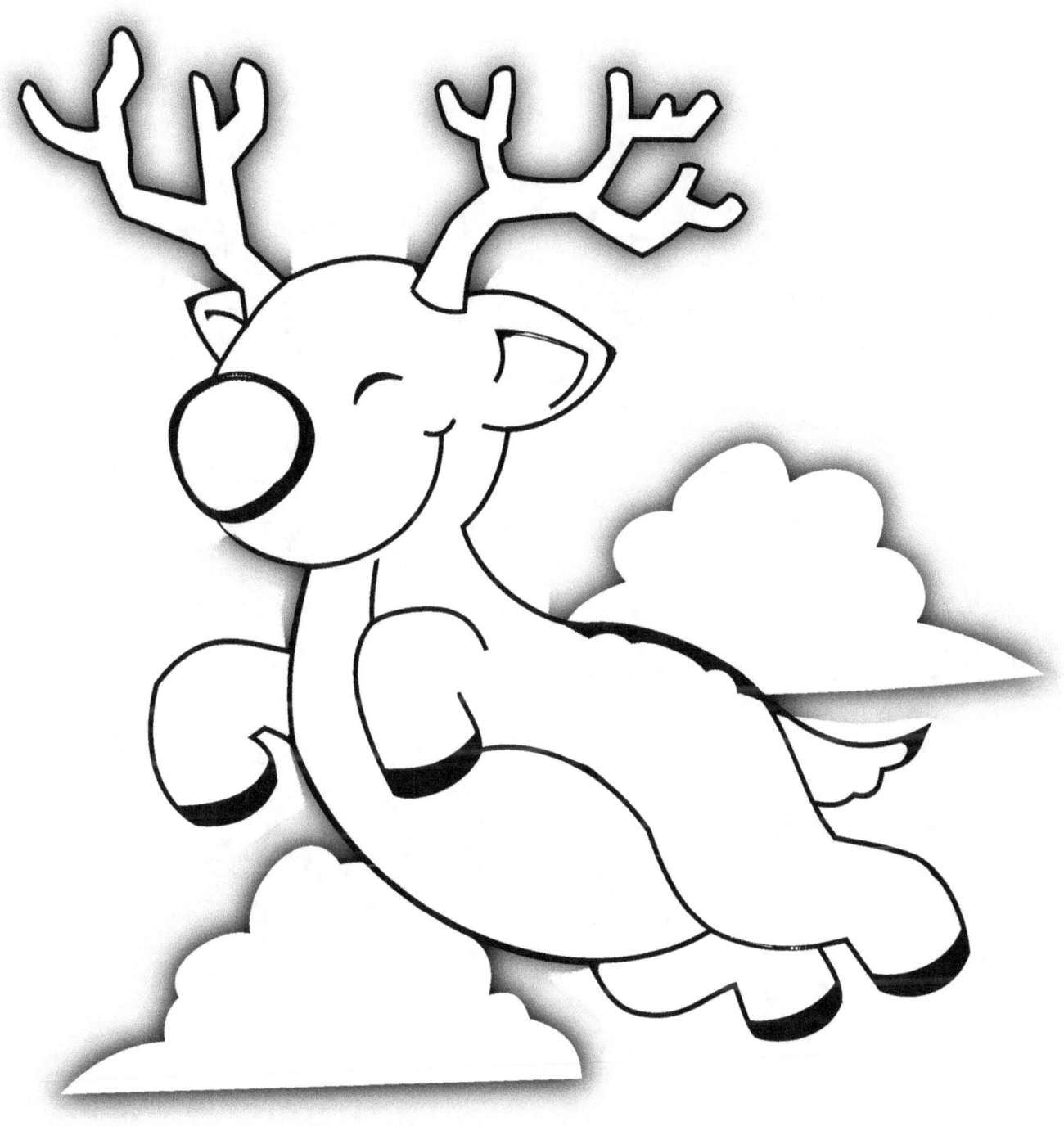

And Be As Good As You Can Be...

Because Santa's Always Watching

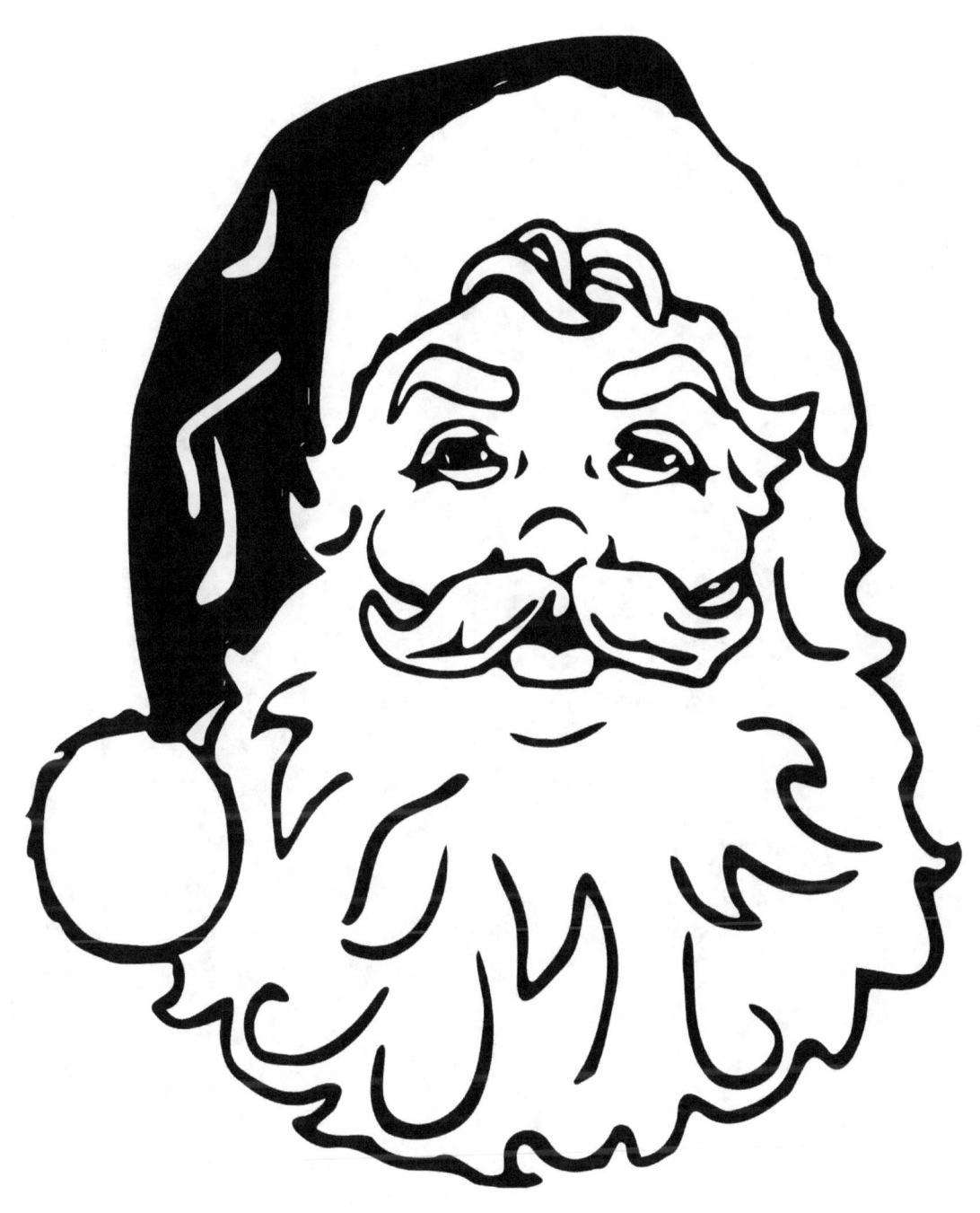

Little Girls And Boys

32

And You Have To Be On
His Good List

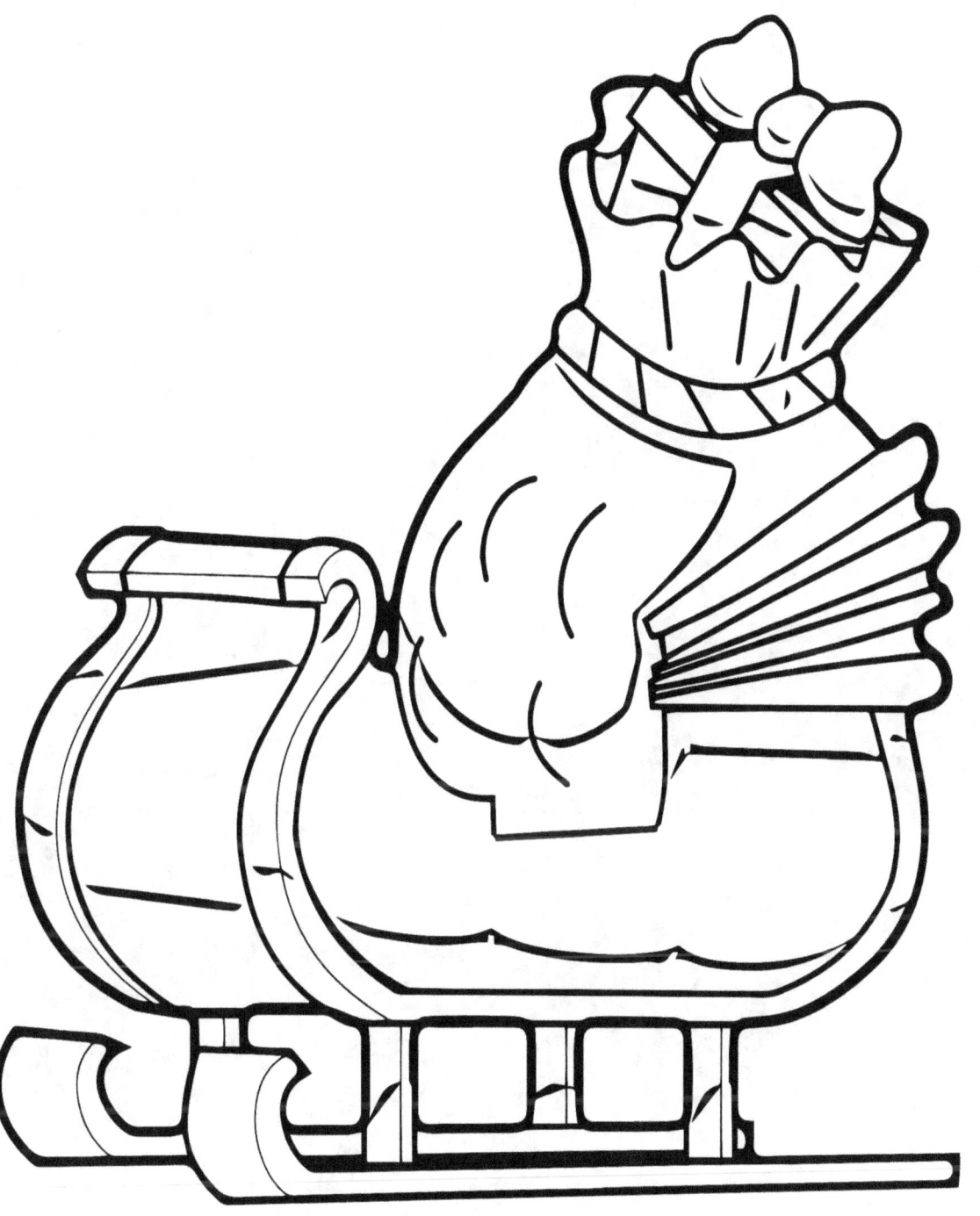

To Receive Your Christmas Toys

Santa Wishes Everyone A
Very Merry Christmas!

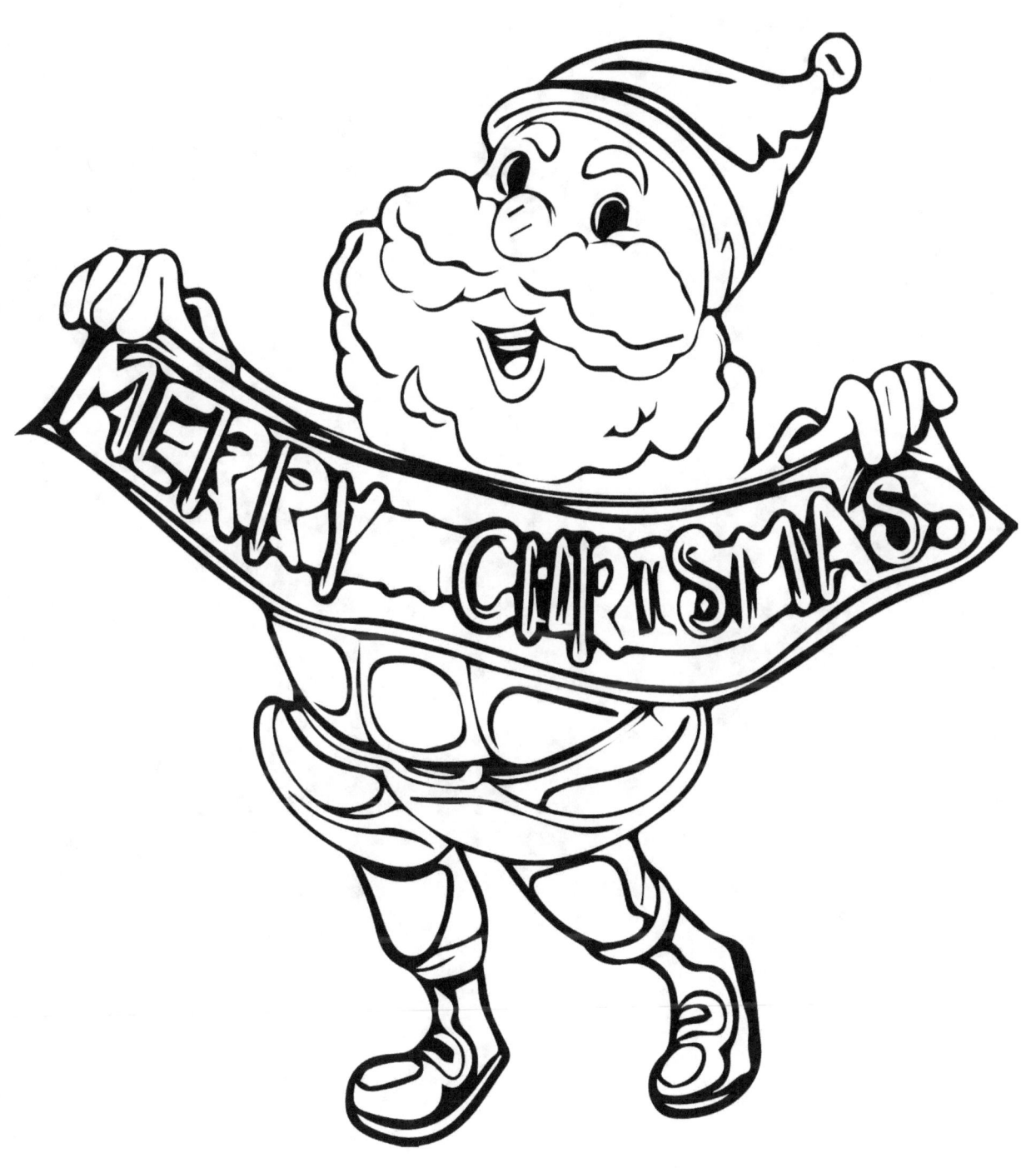

Color The Christmas Wreath
For Your Door

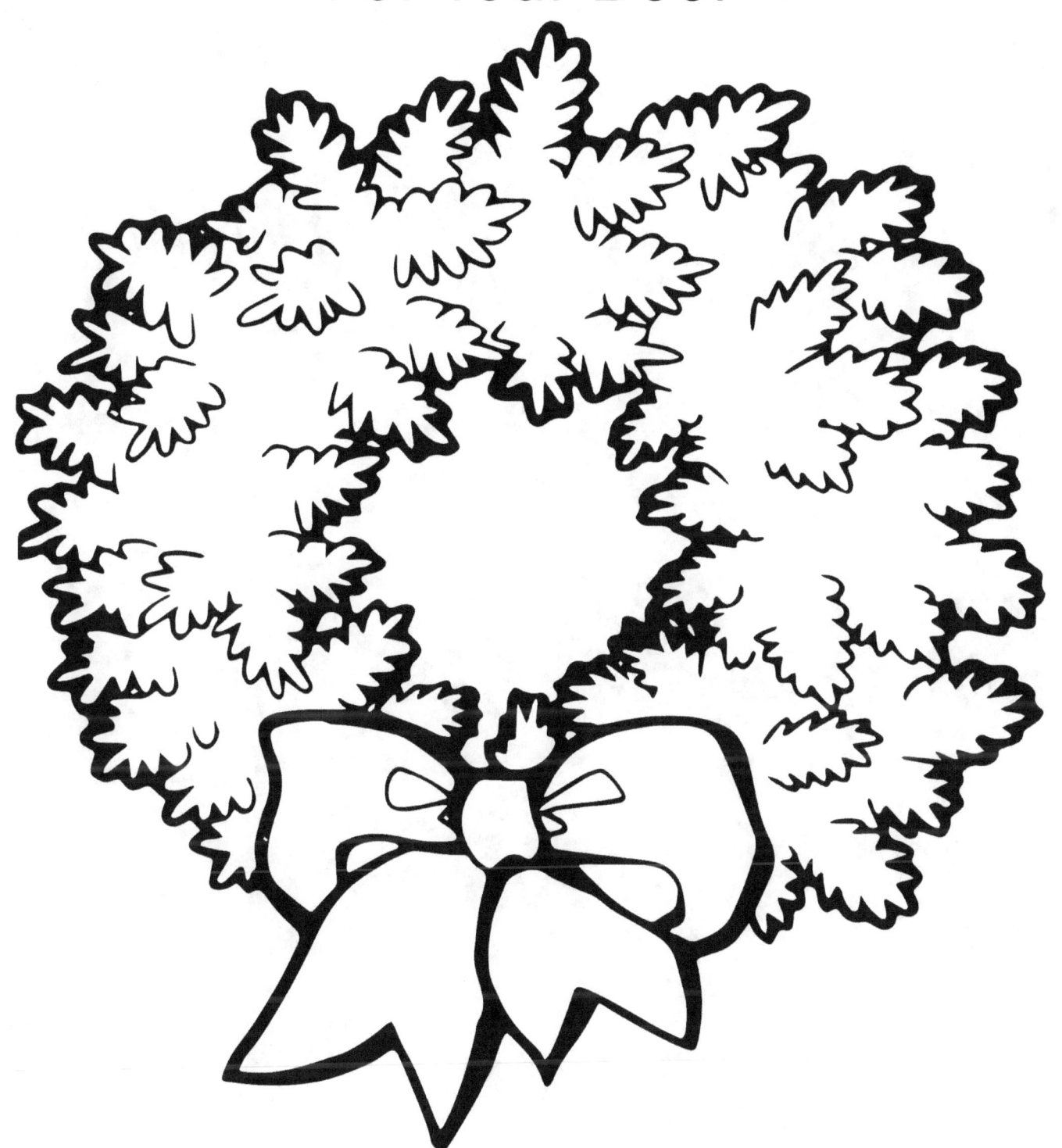

Don't Forget To Draw Some Shiny
Ornaments And A Big Bright Bow!

Santa Can't Travel On Christmas Eve Without His Trusty Reindeer Rudolph

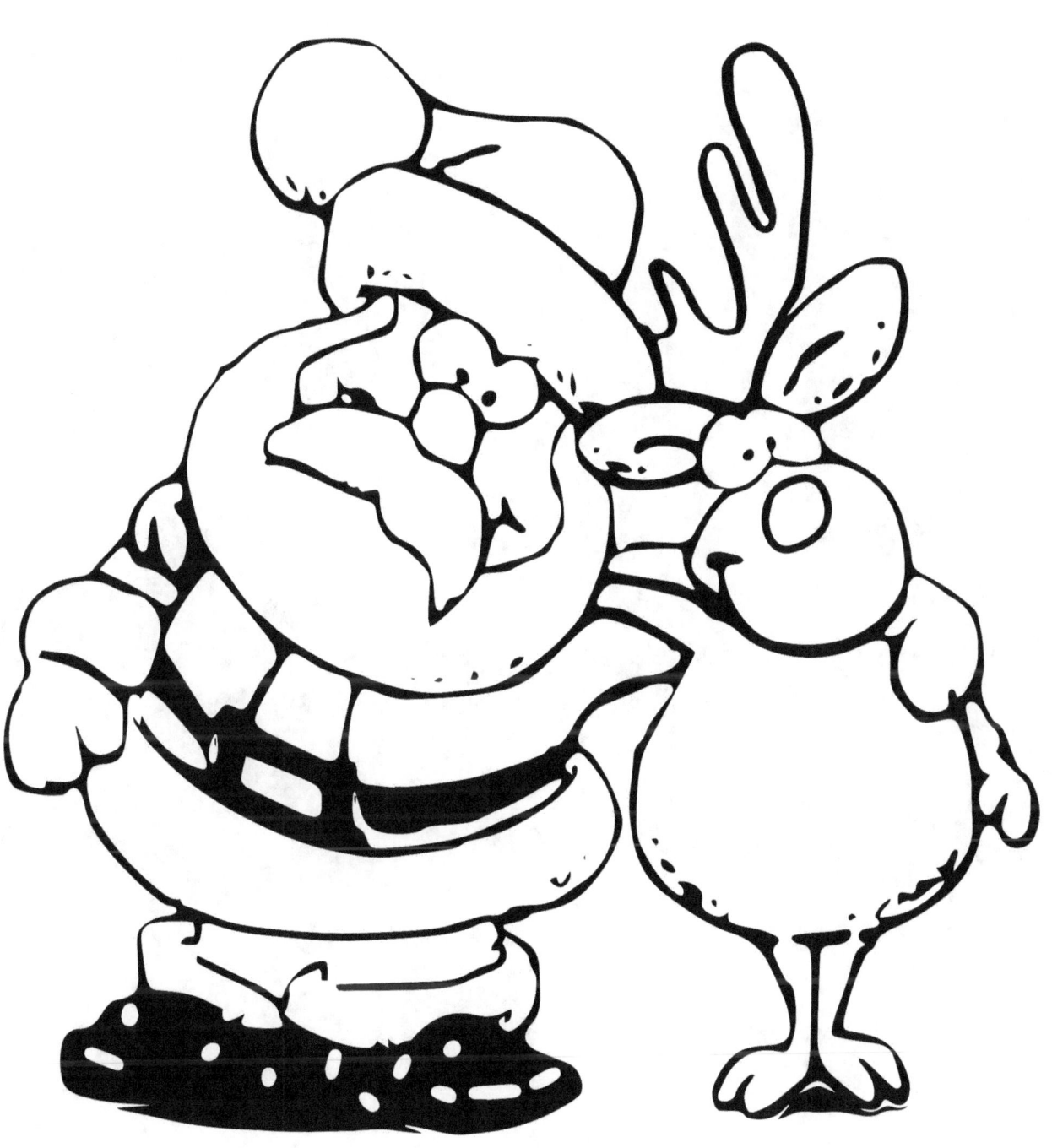

Did You Color Rudolph's Nose Shiney And Red?

Decorating The House Is Fun!

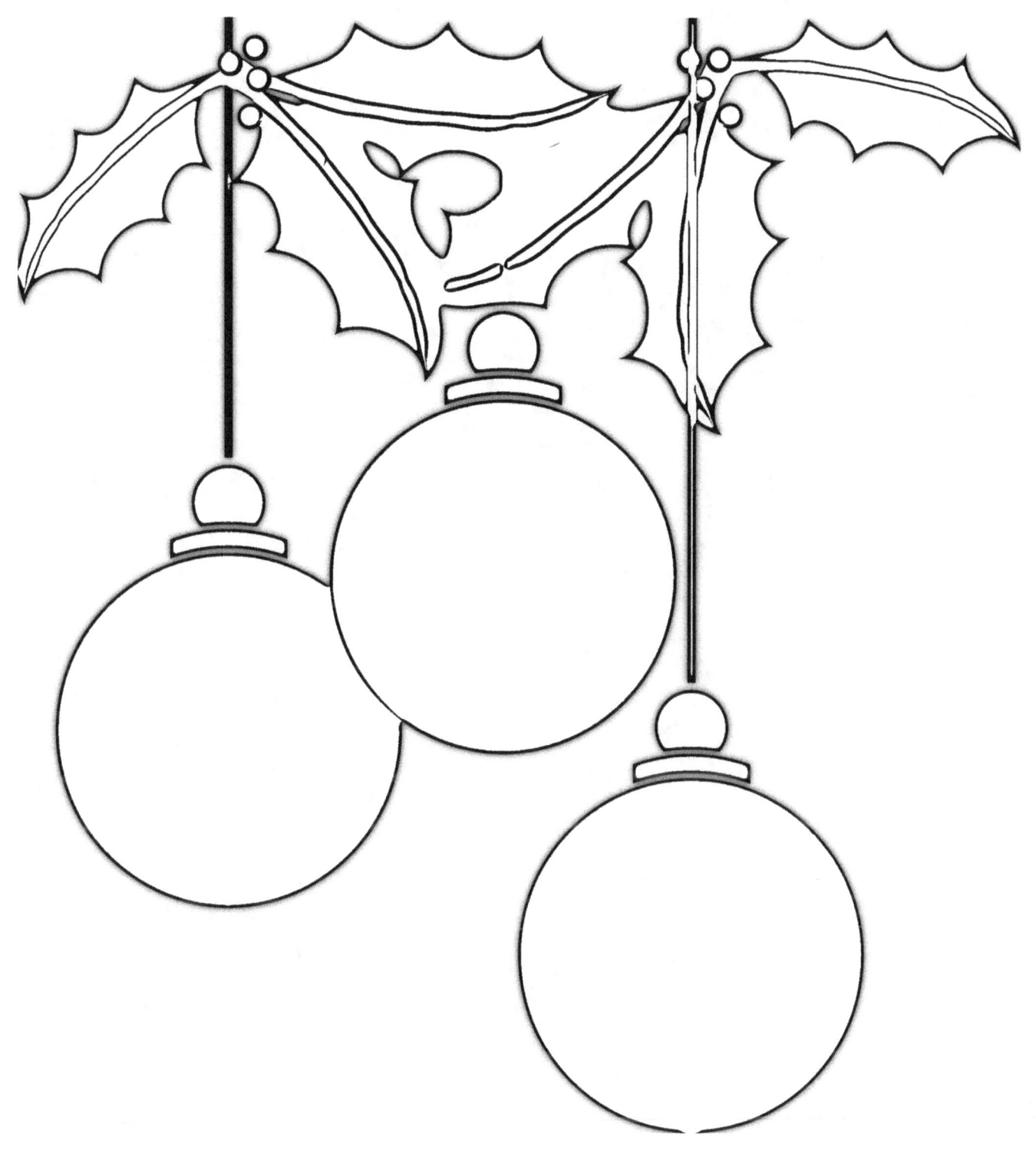

Some Pretty Christmas Decorations.
Make Sure To Color The Holly!

Santa's In A Hurry Getting Toys Ready For Delivery

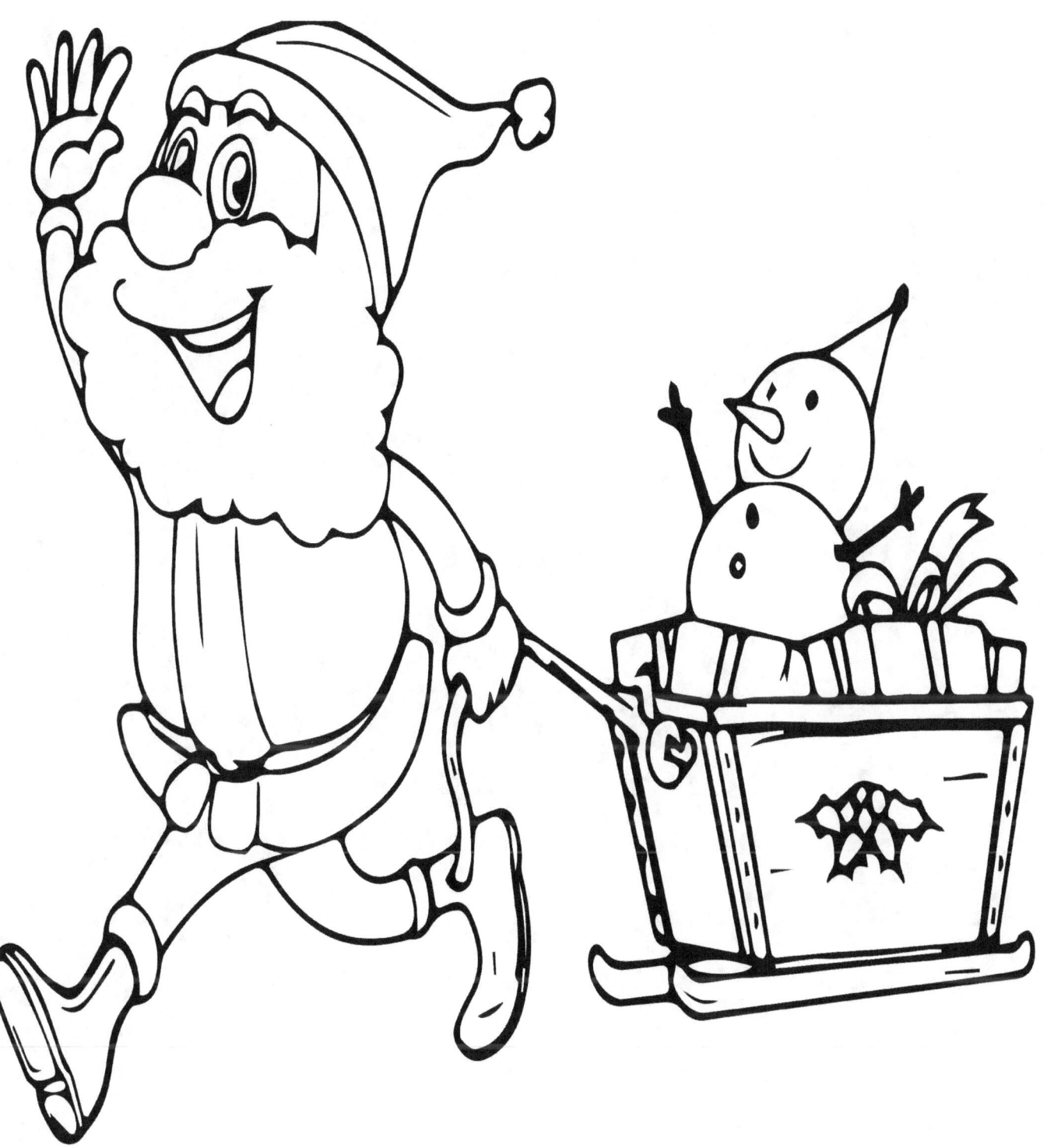

But Always Has Time For A Smile And A Wave!

MERRY CHRISTMAS

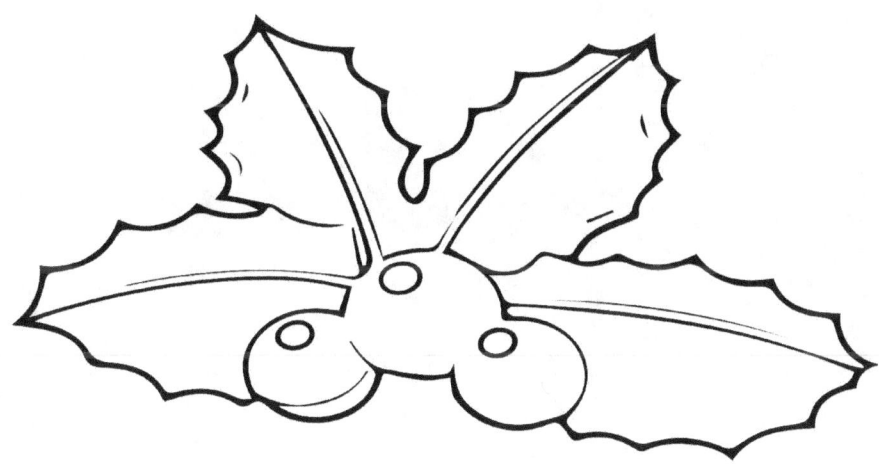

About The
Zen Journal Team

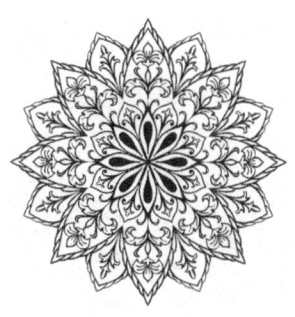

The Zen Journal Team prides itself on producing quality themed coloring books for adults and children alike. This latest title **"Christmas Coloring Book For Kids"** is a children's coloring book that features beautiful kid friendly coloring in designs of some of our favorite Christmas characters.

In 'Christmas Coloring Book For Kids' you will find pictures of Santas, reindeer, teddys, christmas trees, decorations and more that will keep even the most active mind busy coloring in while you get those important Christmas preparations taken care of!

Happy Holidays To Everyone!

Visit us online to download more Coloring Pages and to see our full range of themed Coloring Books:

www.ZenArtworkMandalas.com